Finnegans What?

Lucy Brazier

Lucy Brazier has asserted her rights under the Copyright Designs and Patents Act 1988 to be identified as the author of this work. This book is sold subject to the condition that it shall not, by way of trade or otherwise, be lent, resold, hired out, or otherwise circulated without the publisher's prior consent in any form of binding or cover other than that which it is published and without a similar condition, being imposed on the subsequent purchaser. This is a work of fiction and any resemblance of the fictional characters to real persons is purely coincidental and non-intentional.

ISBN-13 9781092156103
Copyright © 2018 Lucy Brazier

All rights reserved.

Lucy Brazier

CONTENTS

1	I Read Finnegans Wake So You Don't Have To!	1
2	Book 1.1	Pg 3
3	Book 1.2	Pg 10
4	Book 1.3	Pg 17
5	Book 1.4	Pg 24
6	Book 1.5	Pg 30
7	Book 1.6	Pg 36
8	Book 1.7	Pg 46
9	Book 1.8	Pg 52
10	Book 2.1	Pg 59
11	Book 2.2	Pg 68
12	Book 2.3	Pg 78
13	Book 2.4	Pg 85
14	Book 3.1	Pg 91
15	Book 3.2	Pg 98
16	Book 3.3	Pg 105
17	Book 4 - The Final Chapter	Pg 120

FINNEGANS WHAT?

| 18 | The Conclusion - Of Sorts | Pg 128 |
| 19 | About The Author | Pg 140 |

To Samantha Catchpole

Thank you for the Good Ideas (and gin)

I Read Finnegans Wake So You Don't Have To!

But, let me tell you now, this is no insightful academic assessment of what is perhaps the most perplexing, ambiguous and downright impenetrable work of literature known to man. One summer a couple of years ago, in-between writing my own novels of dubious quality, I fancied a bit of a literary challenge. I had participated in Bloomsday - an annual celebration of James Joyce's other famed work, *Ulysses* - a few times and it struck me that maybe it was time to tackle the mighty

Finnegans Wake. The idea of attempting an idiots guide (or, more appropriately, a guide by an idiot) came about after discussing my attempts at comprehension with friends.

And so this, *Finnegans What?*, a plaintive effort to decipher the indecipherable, was born. My method was a to read a chapter and then make notes about what I thought might be happening. These were originally posted weekly on my blog for the benefit of curious readers. So what we have here is a chapter-by-chapter explanation, as I read each in turn. This is my interpretation and musings on Joyce's eponymous work, rather than any kind of instructional companion or serious analysis. Goodness knows, I'm not capable of that kind of high-minded literary endeavour. I'm just an ordinary person, reading *Finnegans Wake*.

And this is what I came up with.

BOOK 1.1

The book starts in the middle of a sentence, which is the second half of the book's final sentence. A chap named Sir Tristam appears to have arrived from America and is riding alongside a river to the town. Not sure what town. I get the impression he is fairly heroic but other than that I can't really gather any more. I'm not one hundred percent sure he is even on a horse, actually.

    I soon realise that it is helpful to recite the text aloud, like a child might when learning to read. It doesn't help me understand it any better but it does give me a sense of rhythm about the thing which changes the experience considerably. It would make an interesting audio book – although there are a lot of words that are unpronounceable and smatterings here and there are written in strange, faux foreign languages. Still – I rather think someone should give it a go.

    A fellow falls off a wall and is killed – this must be Finnegan as there then seems to be a crowd of people around his dead body in a pub. Quite clearly the Wake of the title! I feel quite clever that I have understood a bit of it. Although that's where the comprehension ends, sadly, as what follows seems to be an endless bar crawl interspersed with storytelling and gambling – maybe dancing girls. It is unclear. At this point I have no idea of what's happening or who anybody is, but I put this down to the genius of the writer, recreating the exact same experience of being on an endless bar crawl.

Suddenly we seem to be in the 'museyroom', which I cleverly deduce to be the museum. Or – maybe – a room in which to muse, which sounds nice. Again, I can't really be sure but my best guess is that someone – probably a woman – is conducting a tour. Or she might be on her own and talking to herself. There is some suggestion that Sir Tristam is also the Duke of Wellington. The ambiguous tour guide appears to steal something small from the museyroom and make a run for it. Although it is also possible that she stole from a shop. I get the feeling I am on the wrong track completely, but there is something about this passage that seems important. I literally have no idea.

This is without doubt the most bizarre experience I have ever had with a book but it is oddly addictive. I am aware that I am drifting over chunks of it and keep having to go back, or redeploy the reading aloud tactic.

There then follows a whole bunch of randomness that makes no sense to me whatsoever. I can pick out references to various mythologies and maybe creation stories. Probably other works too but I am clearly not well-read enough to really say for sure. Two interesting fellows called Mutt and Jute meet up somewhere and have a chat. They each enquire as to where the other comes from and agree to swap hats before engaging in dialogue, but I have no idea what they are discussing. There is a reference to someone known as the Prankquean, which is a very promising title. Sadly, I cannot tell you if she is as interesting as she sounds. Let's just assume that she is.

Then we are back in the pub, there is lots of drinking and carousing. Actually it could be a fight. And now I'm not sure if the chap who was dead actually is dead, or if it refers to someone else entirely. Then there is something about a boat.

Thoughts

Well. My immediate thoughts should probably remain unsaid, actually. As you can probably tell, it is incredibly hard to get a sense of quite what is going on. So far, I have no idea which character is which, but even if I did it wouldn't help much as apart from the dead chap I assume to be Finnegan, I couldn't even tell you how many characters there are so far. I am not even sure if they are dead or alive. It is frequently unclear where narrative ends and dialogue begins and the only really obvious dialogue – the conversation between Mutt and Jute – is incomprehensible. Here is a snippet:

Jute: Yutah!
Mutt: Mukk's pleasurad.
J: Are you jeff?
M: Somehards.
J: But you are not jeffmute?
M: Noho. Only an utterer.

J: Whoa? What is the mutter with you?

M: I become a stun a summer.

J: What a hauhauhauhaudibble thing, to be cause! How, Mutt?

M: Aput the buttle, surd.

J: Whose poodle? Wherein?

    And so it continues. It gets even stranger, in fact.

    Joyce uses repetition frequently and there are certainly references to creation stories and the like – I spotted Romulus and Remus (mythological founders of Rome) among the literary debris, which puts me in the mind that this opening chapter is very much about beginnings or origins of some kind. Which is somewhat ironic, considering that the book itself doesn't even have a 'proper' beginning. My observations are by no means definitive and I cannot even be sure that I have interpreted the text at all correctly. But basically, I don't really know what else to tell you apart from I have no idea what's going on. At all.

Favourite Line
'You had a gamier cock than Pete, Jake or Martin and your arch goose of geese stubbled for All Angels' Day'
I bet Pete, Jake and Martin are quite put out at the suggestion of less-gamey cocks!

BOOK 1.2

You will not be surprised to hear that I still have no real clue about proceedings in *Finnegans Wake*, but let's not allow that to hinder us. At last we are introduced to the leading man, (assuming he didn't pop up earlier and I missed it) although even that isn't straightforward. He is Harold or Humphrey Chimpden Earwicker, known more commonly by the nickname Here Comes Everybody or HCE for short. It looks like everyone/thing baring the initials HCE is actually him too, or relates to him in some way. So the main character might actually be lots of people.

Even places. You see? Me either, at first – but one becomes strangely accustomed. Anyway. I think he might be a pirate and there is a King – I think the Sailor King, whatever that is – involved. The King seems fairly friendly with HCE.

There is some discussion of what are either plays or songs that are most charmingly named : *Accept These Few Nutties!, Take Of That White Hat!, Stop His Grog, Put It In The Log* and *Loots In His (bassvoco) Boots* among others.

A little while later there is a paragraph that begins by suggesting that some people have just been described but it is tricky to work out who these are. I will stick my neck out and say one them is Napoleon the Nth.

There has definitely been something occurring in the park – we are made aware of the park by the arrival of *'annoying Welsh fusiliers in the people's park'*, but they are the least of our worries, however annoying they might be. Someone has been up to no good with two young ladies:

"...of having behaved with ongentilmensky immodus opposite a pair of dainty maidservants in the swoolth of the rushy hollow whiter, ..."

It is difficult to tell if the perpetrator is HCE or possibly someone Welsh, but I am leaning towards the former.

After some brief talk of sponges, we seem to be back on the pubs and gambling theme, most probably horse racing. There is a super description of a fellow named Frisky Shorty, who I am fairly sure is a bookie:

Frisky Shorty, (he was, to be exquisitely punctilious about them, both shorty and frisky) a tipster, come off the hulks, both of them awful poor, was out on the bumaround for an oofbird game for a jimmy o'goblin...

It certainly paints a picture. I have also identified another chap who goes by the charming name of Treacle Tom – I can tell you that he sleeps nude in lodging houses but not much else.

    We are then either back on the pub crawl or getting inebriated in general before Joyce – clearly a man after my own heart – ends this chapter on a song, unexpectedly called 'The Ballard Of Pearse O'Reilly'. I do not know who Pearse O'Reilly might be and the song only makes things more confusing. It kicks off as some sort of tribute to Humpty Dumpty, drifts into a verse about horns and butter (no, really) and then seems to almost turn into a different song about someone called Hosty. Hosty has problems with bailiffs and the Duke of Wellington pops up again towards the end.

Unlikely to be troubling the charts any time soon.

Thoughts

I definitely think the key to reading this book is not to focus too much on trying to understand it, rather just let yourself go with the flow. The vast majority of the text I simply don't comprehend at all. But there are definite rhythms to the work that go some way to invoking something akin to understanding, but not in a way that is easily explained. It's bloody weird, is what it is.

I am still struggling to keep track of characters, but Here Comes Everybody is helpfully announced by way of his initials, albeit in sometimes abstract forms. He has definitely been up to mischief in the park with either one or two young ladies, but it is difficult to ascertain exactly what. I wonder if this represents the way gossip is spread around a town; several varying accounts making it impossible to really know the truth.

One thing I have certainly managed to ascertain is that drinking features heavily throughout, at least thus far.

Also, my spellchecker *hates* me right now, I am sure.

Favourite Line

'Fikup, for flesh nelly, el mundo nov, zole flen! If she's a lilyth, pull early! Pauline, allow!'

Great, isn't it? I mean – anything could be going on here. I hope Pauline allows it, whatever it is.

BOOK 1.3

I feel I am getting a bit of a handle on this delightful tome now; the trick is not trying too hard to understand absolutely all of it (or even most of it) rather wait until those rare moments of clarity pop up and read around those. It also helps to look out for the letters HCE appearing in sequence – these bits relate to our main character Here Comes Everybody, or Harold / Humphrey Chimpden Earwicker as he is also known. Talking of characters, there seem to be an endless amount of them. I think some of them are the same person and also some people are lots of other people too. Who anybody is just doesn't seem important. Which is just as well, because three chapters in and I haven't definitively identified anyone apart from HCE.

This chapter seems to be a mishmash of various things all happening at once, quite possibly across different timelines and with varying versions involving an epic cast of people, some of whom flit between life and death with surprising nonchalance. In *Finnegans Wake*, not only does it not matter who you are, being alive or dead is also irrelevant. I am beginning to think that Joyce's characters are related to Schrödinger's cat. Best guess for the opening passage is that a play and actors are being discussed. But there is also a suggestion that false rumours are abound – I am confident that these relate to whatever HCE did or did not get up to in the park. After that, things get pretty confused and several threads are randomly over-lapped and I have to pick my way through the bits I can comprehend. There is no linear storyline *whatsoever*.

Hosty pops up again – it seems he was the composer of the song that closed 1.2 and is described as a musical genius with a good voice. He might have served in the Crimean War, but that could be someone else.

Paul Horan has been jailed. I don't know if this is a recent thing or even who he is or what crime he committed.

Sordid Sam (sounds pleasant) died on Halloween night, it says painlessly but also suggests he was hit over the head. But don't worry, dear reader, he keeps cropping up in the text so for him, death isn't the handicap it might have been.

A whole host of persons are discussed at length but I couldn't really tell you what's going on. They are from different countries and periods in history; your guess is as good as mine as to how they relate to anything else going on, if at all.

Further reference is made to boats and HCE and some kind of evil. Sailors and fishermen feature prominently.

Someone buys a stetson for one and a penny.

There looks like some kind of court case going on (however I later think that this could just be people gossiping in a pub) and I think two of the jury might have died. There is what is described as a 'snappy comeback' from a chap in the 'shoutybox' which I think is the dock:

"Paw! Once more I'll hellbowl!! I am for caveman chase and sahara sex, burk you! Them two bitches ought to be leashed, canem! Up hog and hoar hunt! Paw!"

If that was the comeback, I wish I could work out what said to him.

I now have three theories on what HCE might have done to cause so much discussion:

He raped his friend's wife, making her pregnant with two girls.
He committed manslaughter.
He ran away from a ship in the middle of the night.

But really, the parts that led me to these conclusions could be relating to anyone or could be irrelevant entirely. Still. I am trying.

A tall man carrying a parcel is accosted by a man with a gun, who threatens to shoot him (over a woman), then threatens to shoot his aunt. An altercation ensues, before the following text says that none of this is true, the man isn't tall and there is no woman. So… Okay. No word on the aunt, but I'm assuming she's okay.

An American turns up at the pub wanting a drink, then proceeds to insult HCE for quite some time – *"…weathering against him in mooxed metaphors from eleven thirty to two in the afternoon without even a luncheonette interval..."* which is quite something. There then follows a great rambling list of all the insults hurled at HCE which, although imaginative, do not sound like insults at all. A small sample of the less strange ones are *bogside beauty, york's porker, tight before teatime, archdukon cabbanger* and *Mister Fatmate*.

The chapter ends with a musing about raindrops.

Thoughts

I am finding myself enjoying this book immensely. Not only is it quite unlike anything I have read before, it is also a great deal of fun. The fun is mainly in trying to make sense of any little thing and then the joy experienced when I manage to comprehend something. I imagine a lot of people might not find this fun and it has actually given me a headache on a couple of occasions. But I haven't enjoyed a book so much in bloody ages. Anyway – it is now obvious that there is no linear storyline, no definitive characters and no discernible time line. So many topics are touched on and things alluded to that they are impossible to list. Or even really identify conclusively.

Favourite Lines

'By the siege of his trousers there was someone else behind it – you bet your boughtem blarneys – about their three drummers down Keysars Lane (Trite!)'

'By the siege of his trousers' is now my favourite phrase and I shall be employing it wherever possible.

'Nonsense! There was not very much windy Nous blowing at the given moment through the hat of Mr Melancholy Slow! Probably about a lesser-known Mister Man. It also mentions a hat, which especially pleases me.

BOOK 1.4

This chapter finds our eponymous hero Here Comes Everybody seemingly having a dream that he is dead, or a dream that he is Finnegan (who may or may not be dead, despite the fact he has clearly had a wake). Could be both. There is mention of traitors at the wake and HCE is conscious of enemies, either real or imagined (in this book, it makes no difference!) There features the usual array of incomprehensible rambling that talks about coffins, urns, death in general and a watery grave.

The other main component of this chapter is the court case – which I am fairly sure is actually a court case this time as it mentions being back in the Old Bailey in March. The person on trial is someone called Festy King, who I believe to be an incarnation of HCE. Joyce further adds to the confusion surrounding the crime by talking of *'solving the wasnottobe crime'* and describes someone as being *'associated with the tar and feather industries...'* So not only am I not entirely sure what the crime was, but it is also difficult to tell whether the crime happened at all, or was a heinous attempt to besmirch the Earwicker name. Previously, I thought that a couple of the jury might had died, which is maybe reinforced by Festy being removed at the request of *'a few live jurors'* (as opposed to dead ones). But who knows, really.

Anyway, Festy apparently then murders all the English and leaves the court. The end bit is very confused – it says that the trial is over but then describes four judges returning from their chambers and demanding to see a letter. Not just any letter – a letter that was found by a hen. So, not too specific, then. The chapter closes when HCE's wife, ALP, turns up and recites a poem. Maybe.

Amidst all this, we learn some other interesting things:

Anthony has an unlicensed pig which is later admired by some ladies in a pub. (I am really hoping that 'unlicensed pig' isn't a euphemism).

These pigs are licensed. Probably.

I think a sailor might have been murdered. It could have been Cian, who was murdered in Finntown, but they could be separate people.

If someone steals your ham, you should garrotte them. *Not bad advice, to be fair.*

I think I have identified the ambiguous tour guide from the 'museyroom' in 1.1 – a widow named Kate Strong, whose presence I have now worked out to be distinguished by the word *Tip!* being scattered throughout the dialogue. We also learn that she is some kind of scavenger so I am pretty confident that she did earlier steal something from either the museyroom or a shop. Anyway, she might have been in the park at the time of the crime.

    Back at the wake, a beggar talks to a miner, who is holding a worm.

    Someone threatens someone else with a stick and they fight for a considerable time.

    King Crowbar impersonates a climbing boy (nope, me neither).

Thoughts

    This section was comparatively straightforward, I thought. There does seem to be something approaching a tangible narrative, at least. And my thoughts on characters being interchangeable and indistinct seem to be backed up a little with the line *'Later on, after the solstitial pause for refreshment, the same man (or a different and younger him of the same ham)...'* so I am heartened to know that it really doesn't matter who anyone is. There seems to be a lot of murdering going on, too, which is exciting.

Favourite Lines

'So more boher O'Connell! though rainy-hidden, you're rhinohide. And if he's not a Romeo you may scallop your hat.'
The mention of a hat always pleases me but do you suppose that 'you're rhinohide' is an insult or a compliment?

'That a head in thighs under a bush at the sunface would bait a serpent to a millrace through the heather.'
I think this is a rude bit.

BOOK 1.5

This is the oddest chapter yet. The last one had murders, sex (perhaps) and drama – A bit like an Irish *Game Of Thrones*, but set in a pub. And a courtroom. And everyone is incomprehensible and insane. Anyway. This one seems to centre around two things: a letter and a hen. Let's start with the letter.

It isn't clear who the letter is to, or who wrote it. APL – wife of HCE – is the likely candidate but it is a fact that is doubted by some characters. The letter isn't signed and for some reason ended up on a midden heap, surrounded by orange peel belonging to a child named Kevin. More on that later. As you would expect, the letter is about a great many things and the chapter opens with a two and a half page list of possible titles for this epic work of literature – *Juckey And Dhoult Bemine Thy Winnowing Sheet; Weighty Ten Beds And A Wan Ceteroom; Cotchme Eye* and *A Nibble At Eve Will That Bowal Relieve* being a small selection. There is some superb irony from Joyce throughout as the letter seems to be a reflection of this very book. When the letter is discussed, it ridicules the lack of punctuation and quotation marks and discusses at length how one should not take documents too literally but to look for other meanings. The actual content is only barely touched upon, as most of the narrative focuses on the characters' interpretation of the letter. Sound familiar?

The theme of the crime-not-crime continues and the general feeling seems to be that HCE is innocent of any crime, but maybe there *was* some rumpy-pumpy in the park after all. There are several suggestions as to what might have happened; whilst the pace is light and sing-song, there are some darker concepts touched upon regarding the responsibilities of the ladies in this matter, which are quite distasteful. The juxtaposition is striking and deliberate. However, I like the version of the tale that states that the young lady was angry because HCE ran off immediately after the deed, as he didn't realise how fat and ugly she was without her clothes on. *(It's happened to the best of us, right ladies?)*

Aside from that, it drifts around various subjects including HCE's ancestors, the dangers of listening to gossip, prostitutes and these little gems:

> Bruce has a Scotch spider and Elberfeld has calculating horses. *(Who doesn't want those?!)*

> Brien had a bear paw for dinner.

Annoyingly, some characters have appeared who are depicted by symbols. There is an upside F, a '3' laying face down and a triangle. That's all I know about that, for now.

And then, of course, there is the endless babbling about how the letter was discovered. Which is where the hen comes in.

An inordinate amount of focus is placed upon this hen, who is called Biddy. She is described in glowing terms and heralded as a kind of earth mother, almost goddess-like. Much reverence is given to eggs, and the laying of eggs. Kate Strong *(Tip!)* the widow seems particularly fascinated with Biddy and interrupts discussions several times to talk about her. There is a feeling of disgust that young Kevin left his orange peel on Biddy's midden heap. Maybe Kevin had the letter and he dropped it there at the same time.

The last couple of pages are particularly unlikely all I can pull out is that someone suggests growing a moustache and a chap named Shem the penman comes in right at the end. Could he be the writer of the letter?

Thoughts

Funny little chapter, this. It is jaunty and amusing yet also quite dark, in places. Joyce is fond of repetition and there are a few themes to which he constantly returns, giving the impression that these are the bits he wants you to pay attention to. The attentions placed on the hen and especially the egg are reminiscent of the references to the creation stories earlier in the book, perhaps signifying origins, beginnings and the circle of life.

Themes of uncertainty and contradiction reoccur; whether it be the incident in the park, the identity of the letter's author or the difference between life and death – we are presented with a fact which is soon contradicted by another equally earnest fact later on. And I can't shake the feeling that the Duke of Wellington is significant, somehow.

Favourite Lines

'Now, patience; and remember patience is the great thing, and above all things else we must avoid anything like being or becoming out of patience.'

Especially if we are reading *Finnegans Wake*.

'... flat-chested fortyish, faintly flatulent and given to ratiocination...'

This is a description of someone. I think 'faintly flatulent' is an under-used descriptive term, quite frankly.

'She is ladylike in everything she does and plays the gentleman's part every time.'

A nice little line that actually makes some sense.

BOOK 1.6

Forget what I said about the last chapter being the strangest – this is definitely stranger. I struggled a bit with this one, but I think the overall gist is that this talks about lots of characters and places, through the guise of a pub quiz. It took me quite a while to come to this conclusion as the first question is twelve and a half pages long. I shall do my best to try to convey to you the twelve questions and answers that make up this chapter, but I am pretty sketchy about it all, quite frankly.

Question One: The only reason I have any idea what the question is, is because the answer is Finn MacCool. But for twelve and a half pages, I have no idea what's going on, really. There is a lot of talk of parents, ancestors and far-flung family members across the globe. There are some other points of interest:

There is a shopkeeper (who is also a nobleman) who farts on young boys and likes stockings.

The international convention of Catholic midwives is discussed. Sounds super.

The fairground is a good place to find love.

Someone is a drunk and in love with his mother.

There is a very suspicious-sounding priest who either hates religion or is in some way evil.

Someone has their clothes stolen and is found on Whitehorse Hill with some goats.

A man gets hanged and a gardener comes back as a ghost (not sure if they are the same man).

A group of young ladies are displeased when they are pursued by *'heavy swearsome strongsmelling irregularshaped men'* (But they're the best kind!)

Answer: *'Finn MacCool!'*

Question Two: *'Does your mutter know your mike?'*

Answer: Has something to do with a lady named Ann, who is pretty, flirty and seems to get around a bit.

Question Three: Absolutely no idea what question three is about.

Answer: *'Thine obesity, O civilian, hits the felicitate of our orb!'* (Fat guy falls over? Maybe?)

Question Four: Which Irish city (two syllables, 6 letters) is of *'deltic origin and a ruinous end'* with the biggest park in the world, the most expensive brewing industry, the most well-travelled people and *'the most phillohippuc theobibbous paupulation'*?

Answer: Multiple choice! a) Delfas b) Dorhqk c) Nublid d) Dalway My knowledge of Ireland is woefully poor, so I don't know if this makes sense or not. I think it might be saying that Ireland has the best cities in the world.

Question Five: Another ambiguous one, this. Possibly something to do with the suspect priest from earlier.

Answer: *'Pore ole Joe!'*

Question Six: *'What means the saloon slogan Summon In The House-sweep Dinah?'*

Answer: Could be anything, really, but involves blackcurrant jam, sandwiches and a pot.

Question Seven: This asks about the *'component partners of society'* and lists many examples of these such as *the doorboy, the squeezer, the curman, the mussroomsniffer* and *the bleaka-blue tramp.*

Answer: *'The Morphios!'* I would like this to be the name of a rock band, but probably refers to drug addicts.

Question Eight: *'And how war yore maggies?'*

Answer: Who/what ever the maggies are seem cheerful types and like life, love and laughter.

Question Nine: Possibly asking how a man who has lost his faith views himself.

Answer: *'A collideorscape!'* This question and answer almost approaches some sense.

Question Ten: *'What bitter's love but yurning, what' sour lovemutch but a bret burning till shee that drawes doeth smoake retourne?'*

Answer: There is a very rambling answer which, by and large, seems to be about sex. It is told in the manner of a man and his wife (possibly in bed together) lamenting the long-lost rumpy-pumpy of their youth. There are some quite graphic bits and I heartily recommend giving this section a read. The man is trying hard to get his leg over, but the wife wishes she had married an engineer from a French college. I can't work out if he gets his wicked way, but the overall conclusion is that they are still very much in love.

Question Eleven: Best guess is, it asks if you meet a very odd-sounding gentleman called Jones, would you go to bed with him?

Answer: It starts as a resounding no, and this question is quite an affront! But it quickly gets very confusing and then we are in a classroom setting and our narrator takes pity on us: *'As my explanations here are probably above your understandings, lattlebrattons... I shall revert to a more expletive method which I frequently use when I have to sermo with muddlecrass pupils.'* But things don't get much clearer as we launch into a tale about The Mookse and The Gripes, the former of which is deaf, the latter blind. They are standing on opposite banks of a stream, which then turns into a ferocious river. The Mookse is carrying his father's sword. The stream apparently smells of brown. There is a conversation of some kind, during which the Gripes nearly loses a limb. There is a fight. This strange scene is being watched from above by young Nuvoletta, who tries to catch their attention but is unable. For some reason or another, she flings herself into the river and drowns. The Mookse and The Gripes are each carried off by some women to invisible dwellings and only a tree and a stone remain by the river.

Question Twelve: *'Sacre esto?'* a rough translation would be 'to be doomed'

Answer: *'Semus sumus!'* When we are!

Thoughts

We have departed from courtrooms, parks, letters and heavy drinking and find ourselves trying to solve twelve riddles. I think that this chapter was introducing further information about characters and their histories, but I have to confess to picking up nothing especially useful. Joyce seems to like writing about sex, but I have to say that his style doesn't lend itself well to erotica.

Favourite Lines

'Let thor be orlog. Let Pauline be Irene. Let you be Beeton. And let me be Los Angeles. Now measure your length. Now estimate my capacity.'

Aw. I wanted to be Los Angeles.

'...throughout the eye of a noodle, with an ear-sighted view of old hopeinhaven...'

That noodle's got his eye on you.

> *'Roderick, Roderick, Roderick, O, you've gone the way of the Danes; variously catalogued, regularly regrouped;'*

I like the sound of Roderick.

BOOK 1.7

This chapter appears to be what can only be described as a character assassination of Shem the penman, who is the son of our hero Here Comes Everybody. The narrator is his brother, a man whose name I haven't quite worked out but he seems unusually concerned about the post. He isn't keen on Shem at all and goes to great lengths to tell us why. He might well be jealous of his brother, who is either highly thought of or at least boasts that he is. But he has a dark and hidden past.

    We begin with a physical description of Shem, which doesn't do him any favours. He has a skull, *'an eight of a larkseye'*, a nose, one numb arm, 43 hairs on his head and 18 on his lip, *(which is surprisingly specific)*, three chins, his left shoulder is higher than the right, *'an artificial tongue with a natural curl'*, no feet, a handful of thumbs, a blind stomach and deaf heart, a loose liver, two fifths of two buttocks and a *'manroot of evil'*. The less said about the manroot the better, I think, but the bit about the tongue is very clever.

    When he was a child, Shem posed the first riddle of the universe to his siblings, which is *'When is a man not a man?'* Whoever solves the riddle wins a bittersweet crab, so it is clearly worth some consideration. I lost count of how many siblings are involved but there are a great many rambling and obscure replies that cover just about everything from zombies to prostitutes. When the randomness is finally exhausted, Shem refuses to reveal the answer. Which is bloody annoying.

There then follows a fairly vicious account of Shem's life and his brother portrays him as a drunk, drug addict, gambler, plagiarist and pervert. It seems he is also fond of tinned salmon, tinned pineapple and all manner of foul-sounding food and drink. There is a tale about everyone in town being slaughtered by attackers, while Shem cowardly hides in his house. He also writes bad plays and forges cheques – and wrote an unreadable book – '...*to read his usylessly unreadable Blue Book of Eccles...*' which his brother seems particularly annoyed about.

This is not the first reference to Joyce's other work, *Ulysses,* in this book and it got me thinking. *Ulysses* took place over the course of one day (June 16th, in fact) following the mundane activities of Leopold Bloom. *Finnegans Wake* – where nothing is real, time is irrelevant and persons are uncertain – is very much like a dreamscape and could quite possibly be the single night's delusions of some unknown sleeper. Maybe it will be like *Dallas* and at some point we will be told that it's all been a dream. But anyway.

The insults continue with aplomb and he is described variously as a tragic jester, Shem the evilsmeller, a blasphemer, a loan shark and as a man who has lived the high life and ended up in debt. He is advised to take some kind of medicine to cure him of these ills:

'It does marvels for your gripins and it's fine for the solitary worm'

The chapter closes with the arrival of Shem's mother, Anna Livia Plurabelle (ALP – wife of HCE) who, after some deliberation and general weeping over her sons' arguing, describes herself as a river and sets about defending Shem. We end with these lines, which could mean anything:

'He lifts the life wand and the dumb speak.
-Quoiquoiquoiquoiquoiquoiquoi!'

Other things of note:

On 6th October the Fickle Crowd killed a king.

Shem's brother insists that he take a job, but he won't tell him what the job is, where it is or what time to turn up, only that it involves *'certain agonising office hours'*.

No one dares whiff the polecat at close range.

We are urged to visit Johns Butchers – he used to be a baker, his liver is good value and we are invited to feel his lambs.

He asks Nayman of Noland to make him laugh.

Thoughts

Apart from the fact that the narrator is not a fan of his brother Shem, I haven't picked up anything useful. This chapter has some great descriptive passages and wanders into CS Lewis territory with its beautiful poetic nonsense. Once again Joyce mocks himself by making reference to an 'unreadable book' and I have an inkling that the references to *Ulysses* are somehow relevant. Could this be a sequel?

Favourite Lines

'...and all that has been done has yet to be done and done again,'
Just in case we were in any doubt as to the circular nature of the book, here is a nice little quote to reassure us.

'Oft in the smelly night will they wallow for a clutch of the famished hand, I say, them bearded jezabelles you hired to rob you, while on your sodden straw impolitely you encored'
It's nice to know that one can hire bearded jezabelles, should one need them.

'Shem was a sham and a low sham and his lowness creeped out first via foodstuffs.'
You can tell a lot about a man from his diet, apparently.

BOOK 1.8

This is a pretty odd chapter, even by Joyce's standards. But firstly I can happily confirm that the disgruntled narrator from the last chapter is in fact the hapless Shem's brother – Shaun The Post. I say *confirm*; it is hard to ascertain anything for certain here, but I am as confident as I can be. Shem is a writer and they are both the sons of sort-of-main-character Here Comes Everybody and his wife ALP – Anna Livia Plurabelle.

I spent most of this chapter being completely baffled (no change there, then) but towards the end it came together somewhat. Sort of. As far as I can gather, the passage takes the form of two washerwomen on opposite sides of a river, washing clothes (none too happily, I reckon) and gossiping ferociously about HCE and ALP. This feels faintly reminiscent of the tales of The Moose and Gripes from 1.5.

The details of HCE's extracurricular activities in the park have been published in the local paper and the women chatter away, suggesting that HCE has had many lady lovers throughout his marriage and ALP herself seems keen to run off with either a Lord or a knight, or some chap called Dan. In the much-discussed letter (which was written by Shem on behalf of his mother) ALP apparently discloses that she is a bit fed up with her philandering husband:

'my life in death companion, my frugal key of our larder, my much-altered camel's hump, my jointspoiler, my mammon's honey, my fool to the last December...'

ALP had quite a time of it in her youth – *'She must have been a gadabout in her day, so she must more than most.'* – and some fairly saucy details are salaciously discussed at length by the women. I would divulge further but my mother might read this and it would take me an age to explain it all to her. She apparently has 111 children, (ALP, not my mother) fathered by an impressive array of gentlemen including a tinker, a soldier, a pieman, a policeman, a 'bold priest' and quite possibly the Duke of Wellington (yes, him again!) APL does not remember the names of her children and spanks them with *'the boxing bishop's infallible slipper'*. She also slept with two Scotsmen when she was just a girl, but it is unclear whether this was both at the same time or individually. Also she might wear a wig. ALP is once again described in terms relating to a river, which seems to be a bit of a theme.

Anyway – ALP borrows a mail sack from her son Shaun The Post and nips off in a rowing boat when HCE's back is turned (probably whilst he is trying to work out who is, when he is, and what the devil is going on.) She lets down her hair, takes off all her clothes (something of habit, it seems) and goes into the water *'from crown to sole'*. She then greases the groove of her heel with an elaborate concoction described as an *'antifouling butter-scatch'*. She proceeds to cover her whole body, including *'her little mary.'* ALP makes a garland for her hair with bullrushes and jewellery from pebbles, before embarking on an epic mission to deliver Christmas gifts to all her children – which are now numbered at 1001.

The list of children and their gifts covers two and a half pages, but here are some of the more comprehensible ones:

Chummy the guardsman gets cockaleekie soup.

Isabel, Jezabel & Llewelyn Mmarriage are given a jigsaw puzzle of needles and pins and blankets and shins.

Johnny Walker Beg is gifted a brazen nose and pigiron mittens. *Nice!*

Pudge Craig gets a puffpuff.

Buck Jones is the proud recipient of a prodigal heart and fatted calves.

Sister Anne Mortimer gets a drowned doll. *Not nice!*

Steadfast Dick is given a reiz every morning, which sounds quite good.

There are also gifts for Kate Strong *(Tip!)*, Hosty (he of the ballad-performing fame) and Biddy the hen. Her son Shaun gets a sword and some stamps. Nothing for Shem, apparently he died young.

The last bit of the closing chapter of Book 1 is quite confusing. It looks like a storm whips up and the river becomes torrid. One of the washerwomen turns into a tree and encourages the other woman to die, saying

that they will meet again and part again. I am
sorry to say that I think Biddy drowns. The bats
and field mice become so loud that the women
can no longer hear each other, and as they bid
each other goodnight, they demand to be told
the tale of Shem and Shaun. Even though one
of them is dead and the other is a tree.

Thoughts

This is the final chapter of Book 1 and I
found it pretty tricky, until about three quarters
of the way through. I am pleased that there are
some reoccurring characters that seem fairly
stable – HCE, ALP, Kate Strong and hopefully
Shem and Shaun. There are clear themes that
are visited over and over again – beginnings
and origins, the nature of gossip and rumour
and the unending circle of life and death being
prominent. In the previous chapter, much was
made of Biddy the hen and her goddess-like
Earth mother portrayal. If she is the Earth
mother, ALP is something of an Earth whore, in

the way that the exploits of her youth are unflatteringly discussed by the washerwomen. Sins of the flesh are proving to be another emerging theme. I am fairly sure Freud would have quite a bit to say about this book.

Favourite Lines

'And where in thunder did she plunder? Fore the battle or efter the ball? I want to get it frisk from the soorce.'

I think this is espousing the need to ensure good quality gossip.

'You'd like the coifs and guimpes, snouty, and me to do the greasy job on old Veronic's wipers.'

This just sounds filthy.

'...in a period gown of changeable jade that would robe the wood of two cardinals' chairs and crush poor Cullen and smother Mac-Cabe.'

I think this is about a dress and if so, I want this dress.

BOOK 2.1

Book 2 opens in the form of the program for a play. This chapter seems to suggest that Book 1 was in fact some kind of pantomime and only now do we see the cast and have some sort of explanation as to the plot. We find ourselves in Feenichts Playhouse and are presented with *'The Mime Of Mick, Nick and the Maggies'.* The Maggies have popped up a couple of times before and I am unsure quite what or who they represent but possibly pretty young ladies of some description. As for Mick and Nick – 'Mick' is a slang term for an Irishman and Nick could be 'Old Nick', or the

Devil. But I could be barking up the wrong tree entirely.

Anyway, here are the characters, the name of the actor that supposedly played them and a note of who they represent from the story:

Characters

GLUGG : (Mr Seumas McQuillad) **Shem**. The bad guy. He is in disgrace because he knew too much.

THE FLORAS : (Girl Scouts from St Bride's Finishing School) **possibly The Maggies**. A sprightly bunch of pretty maidens.

IZOD : (Miss Butys Pott) **Ladies in general**. *'A bewitching blonde who dimples delightfully...'* She has jilted Glugg and is now enamoured with his brother, Chuff.

CHUFF : (Mr Sean O'Mailey) **Shaun**. A fair-haired and handsome chap who is the sworn enemy of his brother Glugg.

ANN : (Miss Corrie Corriendo) **ALP**. The mother and lady of the house, married to Hump.

HUMP : (Mr Makeall Gone) **HCE**. A well-dressed and upstanding gentleman, *'having partially recovered from a recent impeachment due to egg everlasting…'*, the cause of all troubles and the landlord of a pub.

THE CUSTOMERS : (Components of the Afterhour Courses at St Patricius' Academy for Grownup Gentleman) **Pub customers / jury**. Twelve gentlemen who drink a lot.

SAUNDERSON : (Mr Knut Oelsvinger) Someone who works in the pub and has nothing to do with the story.

KATE : (Miss Rachel Lea Varian) **Kate Strong (Tip!)** Provides the food at the pub and is a palm reader in her spare time.

The play is set in the present and is described as such: *'With futurist one-horse balletbattle pictures and the Pageant of Past History worked up with animal variations amid ever-glaring mangrovemazes and beorbtracktors by Messrs. Thud and Blunder.'* Right. Apparently, the *'jests, jokes, jigs and jorums'* are lent from the estate of the late Mr T M Finnegan. There then follows credits for a great number of people who put the play together and more information about the play itself.

This would be a good chapter to start with, if one where to think about tackling *Finnegans Wake*. The linear order of the chapters is pretty much irrelevant anyway and at least here we get an introduction to some of the characters and a bit of a clue about what is supposed to be happening. Amid the 'program' itself it suggests that to start at the beginning is madness and requires some kind of divine assistance. It also says that certain parts of the story have been omitted from the play on the basis that they didn't happen. The play closes with the *'Magnificent Transformation Scene'*, when night weds morning and the dawn wakes the world – in other words, it ends at the beginning.

I'm not sure if the next bit is supposed to be the play, or is a scene occurring outside of that, however it is littered with references to Oliver Goldsmith's work *'She Stoops To Conquer'*, another piece based on misunderstandings and mistaken identities. Glugg and Chuff (Shem and Shaun) are vying for the attention of a group of girls. Glugg is having a particularly hard time of it and appears to be conversing with the Four Horsemen of the Apocalypse. It isn't clear exactly but the group seem to be school children.

There is some kind of competition or guessing game, where the prize is dubious-sounding affection from the undisclosed amount of girls present. Whatever the game is, Glugg loses and leaves in disgrace. Isa is sad that he is gone, but reasons that she will soon find another chap to catch her eye. Or a girl, she isn't fussed which. One of the girls appears to be drinking paraffin. They then tease Glugg in song and he pretends to cut off their heads with scissors.

Anyway, Glugg goes away, has lots of fights, does a poo in a river and then goes home. The girls then turn their attentions to Chuff (Shaun), describing him in glowing and affectionate terms. Then Glugg appears to be dead, but rises from the grave when offered sausage and mash – which is rather similar to Finnegan rising up at his own Wake when he is offered whiskey. Eventually, HCE then shouts at the children and tells them to go home for tea. As the chapter closes, the children's game ends and the curtain comes down. They are all sent home to say their prayers.

Other things going on in this chapter:

Someone considers going to Pennsylvania to meet with Mrs Gloria of the Bunker's Trust.

There is a game of strip poker.

Musings on whether or not it is worth killing oneself over poetry. Apparently not. I chose to interpret this part as encouraging those losing the will to live reading this book, not to give up.

The girls' choir sings hymn 29.

Discussion on which houses are better – red brick or wood – and the importance of having a nice letterbox. A great house will be built and it will be the envy of the town.

Chubby will be the chauffeur. Many guests will arrive and sing a song, but they only know the chorus.

Religion again takes a bit of a bashing – there is a bishop who is fond of handsome young men, jibes about how Islam views women and a general suggestion that all religions are equally ridiculous.

The foolish one of the family is at home with Nancy Hands and the dog has run away.

Biddy the hen summons some kind of hen army.

Thoughts

In many ways, this chapter is relatively plain-speaking and if I had read the 'cast list' before I started the book, things might have been a bit clearer. But as is typical with Joyce, just when you think you are getting the hang of his prose, he throws you off kilter once again and I was soon returned to my usual state of merry confusion. Ironically (and no doubt deliberately), the parts where he is earnestly being clear and concise are the parts that cause the most deliberation. Either way, good to see Biddy making a reappearance and taking some kind of positive action.

Favourite Lines

'...*she'll prick you where you're proudest
with her unseat speagle eye.*'
A cautionary tale of getting involved with pretty
ladies.
'*Radouga, ran will ye na pick them in
their pink of panties. You can colour up till
you're prawn while I go squirt with any cockle.*'
This just has to be rude.
'*The swayful pathways of the dragonfly
spider stay still in reedery. Quiet takes back her
folded fields. Tranquille thanks. Adew.*"
I thought this was rather nice.

BOOK 2.2

This is an absolute bugger of a chapter, I don't mind telling you. We are faced with the usual soundscape of narrative that we have come to expect, but it is further complicated by equally baffling margin and footnotes by three different narrators and also some fairly complicated-sounding mathematics. The maths might be straightforward, to be fair, but the combination of Joyce's style and my abject failure to grasp anything numerate prevents me from being anything other than baffled. Nevertheless, I shall do my best.

The narrative appears to be laid out like an exercise or study book, with the main body of text supported by notes:

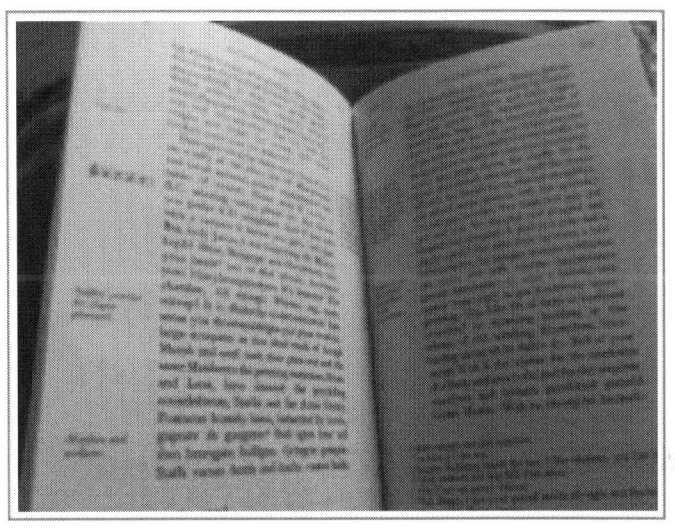

I believe the margin notes to be made by Shem and Shaun, who are here known predominantly as Kev and Dolph. I can't tell whose notes are whose but the righthand ones seem to be taking things much more seriously than the lefthand. The footnotes appearing at the bottom of the page are written by a girl, possibly called Isa, who is a sister or close relative of the two boys. If any of these notes actually relate to the main text, I'm buggered if I can see how.

It seems to follow on from the last chapter and the children have come in from playing and are soon to have tea. In the meantime they are studying a range of subjects including history, science, astronomy, grammar, geography and geometry (more about that later). At the same time they are discussing their father – Here Comes Everybody – running the pub and the drunks he serves. There is some feeling that his regulars are turning against him following the rumours of what happened in the park. There are references to Alice In Wonderland, and dreams and sleep are also talked about, particularly relating to Anna Livia Plurabelle:

'For as Anna was at the beginning lives again yet and will return after great deap sleep rerising...'

Eggs and the now-legendary Biddy the hen are a popular topic also.

The boys are focused on the importance of finding truth and answers (both in their studies here and life in general) whilst Isa muses about love and young men. There is an epic footnote (which could almost be a chapter in itself) which begins with her proclaiming a love of words and literature, but quickly becomes a surprisingly frank account of her sexual fantasies and an angry, graphic demand for her virginity to be taken in quite a specific way. I find this disturbing not only because the age of Isa is ambiguous, but towards the end of the rant, we are very much given the impression that the man to which she is making the demand is none other than her father, HCE.

At various points, pub worker Kate Strong *(Tip!)* pops up to defend HCE and also castigate the twelve customers who seem to be perpetually drinking in the bar. Ships and sailors are once again touched upon (at one point we seem to be simultaneously on both a ship and a pub crawl) and there are references to the earlier parts of the story involving the park and ALP's letter.

Eventually, Shaun and Isa take to berating Shem over his lack of intellectual prowess. Shaun decides to teach him something, urging him to get out his compasses. I think then Shaun begins the lesson, which goes on for ages and is written in derivatives of English, French and Latin. I recognise mathematical terms but really I have no idea what is going on here at all. The upshot of all this is that Shem finally draws a diagram, which Shaun and Isa deem to be a picture of ALP's lady parts.

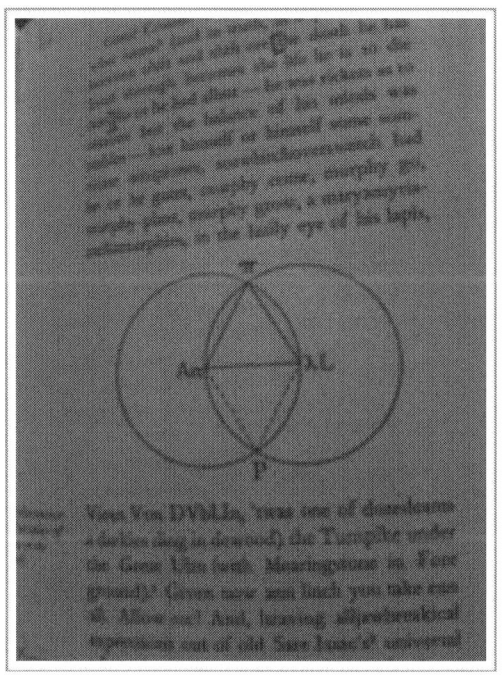

Yep. Clearly a fou-fou.

I get their point, but one would have to have a particular type of mind to arrive at that as a conclusion. Anyway. There follows much talk about the qualities of the feminine intimates and the diagram is admired enthusiastically. It is suggested that it represents ALP herself; her character and history – and maybe women in general. The boys conclude that, in the end, sex and love come to nothing and that the sin is worse than the sinner.

Shem gets angry that he has been tricked into drawing a vagina and strikes Shaun, who responds by taking nearly two pages to compliment him on his punch. They then all drink a pint of Jamesons and praise Biddy's hair. All three return to their homework where they have to write an inordinate amount of essays, which have the kind of outlandish titles you might expect. The chapter ends with them writing a 'Night Letter' to their parents and the patrons of the pub. What they are trying to say, I wouldn't like to presume but it comes across as a sort of threat.

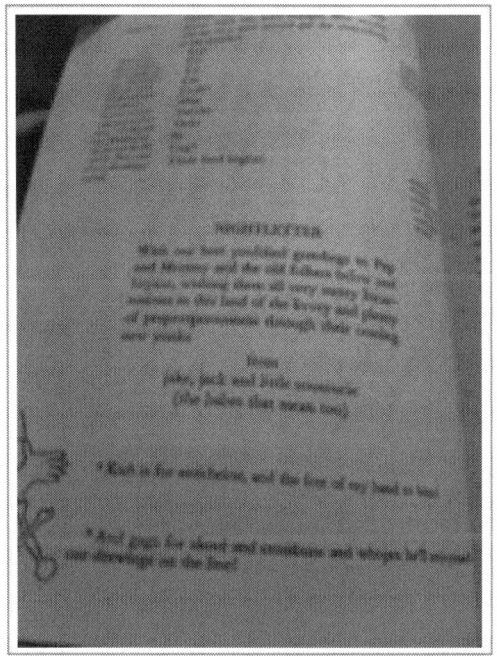

Thoughts

    This is a horrific delight of Joycean contradiction, with some of the most beautiful and humorous prose in the book so far. There are numerous sections of Wonderland-esque imagery which are truly stunning. However, the darker side of this chapter cannot be ignored and Isa's epic footnote in particular is somewhat disturbing. Let's give Joyce the benefit of the doubt and assume that the youngsters are in their mid to late teens, in which case discussions about sex would be expected (although not quite so graphically among siblings, in my experience. But that's just me). Isa's carnal desires are incredibly violent for a young woman and her intention for her father to take her virginity in such a manner is uncomfortable reading.

The placing of these salacious revelations I believe is significant; the footnote is of epic proportions and in very small writing, which may put off many readers from investigating it properly. It is almost as if Joyce is indulging in a kind of confessional that he is partially trying to hide. The religious figures in the book are often portrayed as being deviants and some of the previous references to the possible rape are a little unpalatable to a modern reader. I am no psychologist but this chapter left me with the impression that Joyce harboured some very dark desires that for some reason he felt compelled to share.

Favourite Lines

'Neither a soul to be saved nor a body to be kicked.'

Beautifully tragic.

'... who wants to cheat the chocker's got to learn to chew the cud.'

Conversation is to be encouraged.

'There is comfortism in the knowledge that often hate on first hearing comes of love by second sight.'

For those who don't believe in love at first sight, perhaps.

BOOK 2.3

This bit contains references to some uncomfortable subjects such as rape, incest and paedophilia. Nothing is discussed in any detail, but not everyone wants to read about that stuff and I didn't want to spring it on you. Also there is some swearing from me, just because I feel like it.

This is an absolute bastard of a chapter. For a start, it's nearly 70 pages long, which might as well be in dog years with Joyce's style. It is set in the bar of Here Comes Everybody's pub. The ever-present 12 customers (who are also the jury, if you remember) provide us with one narrative, whilst two other stories are broadcast over a radio and a television, interspersed with a horse racing programme.

The story on the radio is about a Norwegian Captain who has a lobster claw and most likely represents HCE. There are random nautical adventures where people get drunk a lot, someone digs up a corpse, people get shot – that sort of thing. At some point, one of the sailors steals the Captain's *'whale fur'* trousers, but he falls into the sea, taking the trousers with him. Now lacking some trousers, the Captain asks the ship's husband where he can get a suit made, upon which the ship's husband introduces him to a tailor.
The tailor has a daughter who is a proper little strumpet and is no doubt supposed to be ALP. She marries the Captain, then promptly bans him from sailing around the world and forces him to become a pub landlord. At this point, The Captain becomes HCE and starts drinking heavily. Then, someone steals his trousers from the outhouse (There seems to be an

inordinate amount of trouser-theft going on here). Meanwhile, back on the ship the sailors have decided that HCE / The Captain is a rum sort of chap and decide to break into his pub. There is a confrontation where the sailors mock our hapless hero, steal a ham and go off in search of prostitutes. One of them eats a fox and dies.

There is then a weather forecast which is interrupted by Kate Strong *(Tip!)* who enters the bar and starts berating the customers. She then informs HCE that he is wanted by ALP upstairs and off he goes.

The story on the television is about a Russian General, who is known to be a great and powerful man but seems in danger of being brought low by either a lesser man or possibly a child. I think he might be being pursued by the Duke of Wellington, but I'm not completely sure. The Duke of Wellington is definitely involved somehow, though. And also a letter – *'Leave the letter that never begins to go find the letter that ever comes to end, written in smoke and blurred by mist and signed of solitude, sealed at night.'* I imagine this relates to ALP's much-discussed missive.

Now things get quite confusing, so please bear with me. HCE's daughter Isa pipes up and rambles on about men and romance before introducing two radio broadcasters, Taff and Butt (who must be Shaun and Shem). Taff and Butt give warning of a storm, before morphing into Bett and Tipp, who are presenting a programme on horse racing. Slippery Sam is present but morally absent. Taff and Butt return, becoming one person who then shoots the Russian General. *Bastarding bastard thing! This hurt my head a lot.*

We then return to the patrons in the bar. They are discussing HCE's crime in the park and they believe that Shem wrote about his father's crimes in order to discredit him. Whether they mean ALP's letter or another great literary work is unclear. HCE returns from upstairs and his customers turn against him. Faced with the vitriol of his former friends, he then confesses to a liking for young girls and particularly his own daughter. He tries to justify the rape in the park by saying that the young girl enjoyed it and that he had no choice but to commit the act as his wife was refusing him his conjugal rights. He says he was drunk at the time and suggests to the patrons that they would have done the same thing in his position.

Unsurprisingly, a pub brawl ensues and the customers assure HCE that they will all testify against him in court. They also express their intentions to go to the newspapers and bring him down, replacing him with his sons. HCE proceeds to get very drunk on all kinds of drinks and either considers suicide or fears being hanged. He then turns into King Roderick O'Conor, the last king of Ireland (apparently waterproof) and passes out.

Thoughts

Well, this is the best I can do with this chapter. It's an absolute bugger of a thing. And annoyingly it is fairly important, as we finally find out about what happened in the park and also a bit about how HCE and ALP met. The two stories on the radio intertwine with the events in the bar to finally bring the story to something of a turning point. The trouser thefts are a conundrum. Usually when Joyce repeats a theme it is because it's important, but no matter how hard I think on it, I can't see the significance of trouser thefts. Maybe it represents HCE's loss of dignity and public standing.

Finnegans Wake is rumoured to have the longest palindrome in literature, which thus far I can neither confirm nor deny. However, it does have the world's worst knock-knock joke:

'Knock knock. War's where! Which war? The Twwinns. Knock knock. Woos without! Without what? An apple. Knock knock.'

Favourite Lines

'...each spitfire spurtle had some trick of her trade, a tease for Ned, nook's nestle for Fred and a peep at me mow for Peter Pol.'
A commentary on the local prostitutes.

'...(pierce me, hunky, I'm full of meunders!)...'
Not sure when one would use this phrase, but it sounds quite good.

'And then. Be old. The next thing is. We are once amore as babes awondering in a wold made fresh where with the hen in the storyaboot we start from scratch.'
The circle of life and… Biddy!

BOOK 2.4

This chapter is a sort of dream sequence, quite possibly of our now shamed hero Here Comes Everybody, as we left him unconscious on the pub floor at the end of Book 2.3. There seems to be little connection to the main story, but that is probably true about most of the book anyway. It opens with a poem about a chap named Mark, who loses his shirt and trousers in a dark park. He appears quite full of himself and is described in the poem:

'You're the rummest old rooster ever flopped out of a Noah's ark
And you think you're the cock of the walk.'

But apparently he isn't the cock of the walk, that accolade goes to Tristan, the young fellow of legend, who is wooing the beautiful maiden, Isolde. Whilst they go about the general business of being lovers – including canoodling on a fifteen inch love seat – they are watched secretly by four dirty old men, known as the Four Masters. They are:

Matt Gregory – wears a 'saltwater hat' and is a 'queenly man'

Marcus Lyons

Luke Tarpey – possibly Welsh

Johnny MacDougall – wears half a tall hat. The other half he lost to someone called Lally, who also took other belongings from him.

The Four Masters seem to represent Matthew, Mark, Luke and John whilst also being related to the four elements of earth, wind, fire and water. They are old men, all divorced by their 'shehusbands', who reminisce endlessly about their own past conquests and the many lovers who have left them. As they spy on Tristan and Isolde, they repeat themselves constantly about their memories, which revolve around women, education, the great flood, auctioneers and drinking.

The theme of repetition is presented as the Four Masters (and mankind in general) being destined to repeat the same mistakes:

'...when hope was there no more, and putting on their half a hat and falling over all synopticals and a panegyric and repeating themselves...'

They eventually implore the Almighty to release them from this cycle so that they are able to die – which they eventually do (*'happily buried'*), having forgotten all their memories.

Meanwhile, we are presented with some sort of alternative creation story and tales of a lot of people dying at sea. The education system is mocked and there is a bearded Queen who has various dealings with Roneo and Giliette. These two undoubtedly reference Romeo and Juliette, but I can't help thinking it would be better if it was Gillette; not only could the bearded Queen sort out her face fuzz, but she could claim to be 'the best a man can get'. Anyway.

HCE laughs at Welshman Tom Tim Tarpey and four middle-aged widowers, who are no doubt the Four Masters.

A woman plots to kill a man (possibly HCE) with a pair of borrowed curling tongs.

Biddy is writing her memoirs, which are being serialised in Grocery Traders Monthly magazine! (Someone should really write some fan fiction based around this, I think).

The chapter – and, indeed, Book 2 – ends with a poem about Tristian and Isolde, in which he proposes to her and she accepts. But, in line with the much-recounted legend of old, the suggestion of an undisclosed tragic ending to their tale looms large.

Thoughts

I have various thoughts about what this is all about, but they are pure conjecture. Repetition is a device that has been employed liberally by Joyce since the beginning and there are two purposes for this of which I am certain. The first is to draw the reader's attention to aspects of the tale which are important. The second, I believe, is to evoke particular feeling and atmosphere within the reader. Often the words of a passage are irrelevant and it is the soundscape they create upon the tongue and mind where the meaning is found.

There is no concrete reality or true narrative in *Finnegans Wake*, making it impossible to tell unconscious from conscious thought and truth from gossip, rumour and myth. In some ways this makes it the most realistic of novels as real life is endlessly interwoven with our different perspectives and understandings of people, events and the world at large. It makes for bloody complicated reading, though.

Favourite Lines

'The new world presses. Where the old conk cruised now croons the yunk.'
Even if I knew what a conk and a yunk were, it still probably wouldn't make much sense.

'...and he was so sorry, he was really, because he left the bootybutton in the handsome cab and now, tell the truth unfriend never,'
I would be sorry to misplace a bootybutton, for sure.

BOOK 3.1

Following the rather grim close of Book 2, we find Book 3 in a much jollier mood. The upbeat narrator of this first chapter is a donkey owned by the Four Masters. We open with the donkey falling asleep at midnight as a church bell sounds. The donkey dreams that he sees Shaun, dressed like an earl and looking fabulous. He is a fan of Shaun and extols his skills as a great postman. Shaun then embarks on an epic eating spree, starting with a breakfast that includes a steak stolen from a black bat. There follows dinners of many courses and every kind of victual you can't imagine. Shaun gets bigger and bigger and is very pleased about the fact.

The donkey then hears Shaun speak – he appears to be addressing a crowd and waving an axe. Shaun brushes his teeth before talking at length about how great he is and how he alone was entrusted to deliver ALP's letter. He is then questioned by an unspecified amount of anonymous sycophants, who are as obscure in their inquiries as you would expect. They begin by asking who gave him the letter to deliver, to which he offers a prompt denial of ever being anywhere near the letter, actually he isn't a postman and in fact he works in a factory. The simpering inquisitors are unconvinced and politely call him a liar, forcing him to eventually admit to delivering the letter. When they press him further about the contents of the letter, Shaun distracts them by complaining about bad pastry before launching into a series of brilliantly random excuses as to why he does not know details of the letter.

Shaun creates a distraction by berating his brother Shem, who is now confirmed as the author of ALP's letter. He claims Shem forced ALP into saying awful things about her husband HCE in order to discredit him. Shaun declares the letter to be all lies, and poorly written lies, at that. This is just one of many insults thrown at poor Shem, which are frequently very funny. A couple of my favourites:

'You know he's peculiar, that eggschicker, with the smell of old woman off him, to suck nothing of his switchdupes.'

'He's weird, I tell you, and middayevil down to his vegetable soul.'

'Then he was pusched out of Thingamuddy's school by Miss Garterd, for itching.'

Interestingly, Shaun also claims that Shem has been forbidden from mating by HCE.

At some point, Shaun appears to find himself in a barrel floating in a river. Not sure quite how or when this becomes a thing, but it's quite important nonetheless.

A further distraction is a very elaborate saucy tale involving a grasshopper, which quickly becomes a weird kind of insect erotica, and is absolutely one of the most bizarre things I have ever read. Shaun also sings a song about the grasshopper, whilst stuffing his face with more unlikely-sounding food.

The questioners praise his story telling skills, before asking him again about the letter. Shaun responds by speaking highly of his own writing and comparing himself to Oscar Wilde. Eventually, Shaun tells us when the letter was written:

'When she slipped under her couchman. And when he made a cat with a peep.'
And also this:
'Letter, carried of Shaun, son of Hek, written of Shem, brother of Shaun, uttered for Alp, mother of Shem, for Hek, father of Shaun.'

Looks like the brothers share a mother but HCE is the father of Shaun only. Perhaps this explains the animosity between them.

Unrelenting in their quest for the truth about the letter, the questioners press for more details, to which Shaun responds with delightful ramblings and manages to avoid giving any answers at all. He then falls out of the barrel and into the river, being swept away to either his death or Biddy's house, possibly both:

'Wisha, becoming back to us way home in Biddyhouse on way or either anywhere we miss your smile.'

Shaun then simultaneously dies and leaves the donkey's dream.

Thoughts

This is a great chapter! It is a jaunty merry-go-round of the beautifully put questions, fabulous rambling excuses and tall tales involving a myriad of eclectic characters and long-awaited information relating to HCE and family and also ALP's letter. We wander quite firmly into Monty Python territory here, with great pieces of witty absurdity and surreal humour. I have noted far more 'favourite lines' than is reasonable to list here. If you only attempt one part of *Finnegans Wake*, I heartily suggest having a crack at this chapter. There is the usual mush of the undecipherable but there are also plenty of bits that are highly enjoyable with only a little bit of wrestling.

Although I suspect Shaun is an unreliable narrator, he does confirm some aspects relating to the letter and the family and also reveals a lot about his own boastful and decadent character. We are again presented with the themes of dreams, rivers and the legendary Biddy – symbol of the circle of life. Cheerful stuff all round.

Favourite Lines

'I've no room for that fellow on my fagroaster, I just can't.'
Always a disaster when there's no room on the fagroaster.

'We shall not come to party at that lopps, he decided possibly, for he is not on our social list.'

Shaun is selective about where he parties.

'To The Very Honourable The Memory of Disgrace, the Most Noble, Sometime Sweepyard at the Service of the Writer.'

There is just something very majestic about this, somehow.

BOOK 3.2

Shaun returns to reality (if you can call it that) from the donkey's dream, going by the name Jaunty Jaun, a man know *'far and wide, as large as he was lively, was he noted for his humane treatment of any kind of abused footgear,'* . He seems a little roughed up or worse for wear. He passes a policeman who has fallen asleep, drunk, at his post and eventually comes across his sister Izzy (Isa from previous chapters) and 28 schoolgirls from St Brigid's School sitting under a tree. They are apparently learning *'their antemeridian lesson of life.'*

Jaun greets the schoolgirls with a doff of his hat (with a reinforced crown) and they all make a great fuss of him – all except the prettiest girl. The girls jiggle his fat, feel his manhood and declare him to be sixteen years old, which is rather forward of them in several respects. In return, Jaun makes various comments on their appearances (some quite harsh, others salaciously approving) and advises them to read up on Irish legends.

It appears that Jaun is planning on going away and speaks fondly of his sister Izzy, declaring that he will miss her terribly. He then goes on to discuss a sermon he heard given by Father Mike and implores the girls to gather around and listen. It is quite a lengthy sermon, as it turns out. It starts off innocuously enough, with instructions to keep the Ten Commandments, go to church on a Sunday and not to eat pork on a Friday. There is practical advice about cooking (the importance of food is greatly stressed) and keeping a clean house, plus some very useful tips on handling an alcoholic husband – which if they end up marrying any of the characters from this book could come in very handy. Jaun preaches the importance of remaining chaste and virtuous, but expresses this in such a suggestive manner that you very much get the impression that he prefers the company of somewhat less virtuous ladies. To further this point, he gives some quite detailed and graphic advice on lovemaking, although one wonders how a chubby sixteen year old has accumulated such esoteric knowledge. Other highlights of the sermon include:

'Never lose your heart away till you win his diamond back' (I think this is tip for card games)

Warnings about posing nude for artists

Don't sleep with a piano player, especially if he is your lodger

'Never park your brief stays in the men's convenience. Never clean your buttoncups with your dirty pair of sassers.' Wise words indeed!

There is also what appears to be a swipe at his mother, ALP, when he explains at length the error of cheating on a husband with a great many men and becoming pregnant. Jaun generally speaks highly of his mother in both this chapter and the one previous, but his hatred of his illegitimate half brother Shem is evident throughout the book.

Eventually, Jaun announces that he is hungry and needs to go. He asks the girls to wait for him until the *'grame reaper'* comes, but Izzy has other ideas. She implores him not to leave and starts talking about priests. Another of the girls declares her love for Jaun, but sadly cannot pursue her feelings for him as she already has a boyfriend who is more gifted in the trouser department. Unimpressed, Jaun has a drink and starts shouting. He tells the girl that she can have Dave the Dancekerl instead. Jaun is very fond of Dave:

'I bonded him off more as a friend and as a brother to try and grow a muff.'

As luck would have it, Dave comes around the corner carrying some pate and three white feathers. Jaun proceeds to sing his praises, although there are a few snipes about his physical appearance – Dave is far more slender than Jaun and I think he is a bit jealous about the fact.

Jaun insists that he must board a ship immediately and all the girls weep with despair. Then, a worrying thing. These words appear:

'But the strangest thing happened.'

Considering the unlikeliness of the book so far, one can only wonder with ever-increasing dread what it might mean by 'the strangest thing'. As it turns out, I don't have much of an idea, unfortunately, except that Jaun chokes, spits and curses. A great deal of randomness ensues and Jaun possibly dies. We end on this note:

'The silent cock shall crow at last. The west shell shake the east awake. Walk while ye have the night for morn, lightbreakfast-bringer, morroweth whereon every past shall full cost sleep.

Amain.'

Thoughts

This is a very amusing and quite naughty chapter on the whole but the overall feeling is one of hypocrisy. The boastful Jaun / Shaun presents himself initially as a wise and pious fellow, to whom the young ladies should pay great attention. But he immediately abuses his position by endlessly detailing the behaviours he at first advised them to avoid. Joyce has a marvellous sense of irony and makes flagrant use of juxtaposition to create some very dark humour. On the upside, the final lines suggest that someone is on the way with some breakfast, so it's not all bad.

Favourite Lines

'I'll tear up your limpshades and lock all your trotters in the closet, I will, and cut your silk-skin into garters.'

Now, there's a threat if ever I heard one.

    'And is that any place to be smuggling his madam's apples up? Deceitful jade. Gee wedge! Begor, I like the way they're half cooked.'

I don't know what it means but it made me laugh.

    'Dress the pussy for her nighty and follow her piggy-tails up their way to Winkyland.'

Quick trip to Winkyland, anybody?

BOOK 3.3

As we approach the end of this phenomenal work of insanity, the chapters seem to get longer and more dense. There's a lot going on in this one and – as usual – it is pretty obtuse. But we'll give it a go.

Shaun (here referred to as 'Yawn') wakes up wailing on a hillock *(well, we've all done it)*:

'His dream monologue was over, of cause, but his drama parapolylogic had yet to be, affact.'

He appears to have a raging hangover and is in a proper state. Then, three kings from the East Midlands show up, accompanied by the Four Masters from previous chapters. It could be that the three kings and the Four Masters are the same people somehow. Who knows. The donkey is with them, lurking at the back, when they come across Shaun laying among the poppies. After an inordinately complex conversation, they decide to wake Shaun so that they can question him.

Shaun awakes and there ensues a typically confusing conversation that swings back and forth between many topics. It is often ambiguous as to who is speaking and Shaun seems to become HCE at times. A discussion about an orangery soon turns into talk of letters and in particular, the famous missive that may or may not have been written by ALP:

'This nonday diary, this allnights newsreel.'

Shaun is accused of causing scandal about the letter, and even of writing it. He responds by saying that someone is impersonating him, blaming his half-brother Shem. The Masters challenge Shaun over his claims to be a good and pious man and remonstrate with him about his poor treatment of Shem. Shaun offers an unconvincing account of fraternal love, then has some kind of vision which causes him to have a funny turn.

There is also a missing boat – it is orange – and it is possible that the Duke of Denmark ate it.

The Masters and Shaun then embark on epic discussions about ALP, the wake, HCE's pub and various things that may or may not have happened. Eventually, they all get excitable and start shouting over each other. Some kind of spirit or ghost pops up (could be HCE but might also be the Prankquean from Book 1) and talks about the infamous events in the park. HCE is declared a drunk and bad husband, also *'As mad as the brambles, he is.'* The spirit then talks of kissing HCE, which makes the Masters somewhat cross. There is also some anger about a shapeless hat, but I'm not sure how that's relevant.

We then seem to be back at the wake of dear Finnegan, where the priest is sober but everyone else is drunk and wanting to fight. Mr Magraw beats someone up while HCE goes in search of ALP, feeling amorous. She rebuffs his advances which HCE finds very unfair as she is apparently not refusing the affections of others, particularly Big Arthur. The infamous pub crawl is relived with gusto, as well as many other events from the book. Eventually someone gets shot and Shem is also murdered.

One of the Four Masters challenges the other three to a fight. HCE gets annoyed at being questioned and launches into a defensive and whining account of his whole life. This is effectively another retelling of the entire book, but from a point of view much more sympathetic to HCE. Essentially, ALP, women and drink are blamed for his shortcomings and the Masters eventually concede that he is 'more sinned against than sinned'.

HCE then appears to be conversing directly with ALP, forgiving her for her adultery:

'Still to forgive it, divine my lickle wiffey, and everybody knows you do look lovely in your invinsibles,'

He also tells her that she should never have entered his dream. There appears to be an attempt at copulation (amusingly referred to as a game of hunt the orchid) but ALP keeps interrupting proceedings by gossiping and talking general nonsense. She discusses the departed Finnegan:

'His thoughts that wouldbe words, his livings that havebeen deeds,'

and we learn that he was fond of women and drink. Quite frankly, you are hard pushed to find anyone not fond of women and drink around here.

There is a final, plaintive protest of innocence from HCE (including an interesting defence for the crime in the park, revolving around the effect excess alcohol has on a gentleman's trouser performance), mainly blaming Shem and Shaun for spreading rumours, his friends for turning against him and ALP for breaking his heart.

As we end the chapter, dawn breaks and the donkey and Biddy wake up.

Thoughts

This is a very sketchy outline of what is an extremely long and complex chapter. There is so much going on here and we get HCE's life story at least twice, from differing perspectives. I have to say that it's not the most fun chapter, despite there being lots of points of interest, mainly due to its density and the fact that it goes on and on. And we are not really any closer to knowing anything concrete about the characters or the events that involve them.

However, the detailed retelling of the pub crawl is very entertaining and seems to get more violent and obscene with each recount.

Favourite Lines

'...not even to the seclusion of their beast by them that was the odd trick of the pack, trump and no friend of carrots.'
Is anyone really a friend of carrots? Really?

'The old order changeth and lasts like the first. Every third man has a chink in his conscience and every other woman has a jape in her mind.'
Sort of interesting, don't you think?

'Who kills the cat in Cairo coaxes cocks the Gaul.'
Let that be a lesson to you.

'God bless your ginger, wigglewaggle! That's three slots and no burners.'
Just loving the thought of a ginger wigglewaggle.

BOOK 3.4

The penultimate chapter of *Finnegans Wake* sees us back on relatively familiar ground with yet another perspective on the ambiguous events from the tale. We find ourselves in the company of the slumbering Porter family, who appear to be an alternative version of the Earwickers – Here Comes Everybody's dysfunctional brood. The Porters are portrayed as being the perfect family, although they only care about themselves.

It is nighttime and the three children are asleep upstairs. They are:

Jerry – drinks methylated spirits and wants to grow up to be a bald cardinal.

Described as a *'badbrat'*, he is reminiscent of Shem.

Kevin – Shaun has already appeared once before as Kevin and here he apparently grows up to be the *'commandeering chief of the choirboy's brigade'*.

Isobel – No doubt representing the promiscuous Isa, Isobel is the chaste and beautiful sister of Jerry and Kevin who yearns to be a nun.

The first part of the chapter appears to depict the dream of Jerry and concerns HCE's court case. We hear again HCE defend his crimes, this time citing some sort of medical problem, but is eventually found guilty by the jury. On leaving the court house, Jerry sees twenty nine young girls (who are never happier than when they are miserable) weeping over the departure of Shaun.

We then find ourselves the bedroom of Mr and Mrs Porter, which is situated above a pub. The description of the bedroom is wonderfully vivid, so I thought I would include the passage here, should you wish to have a peek at it:

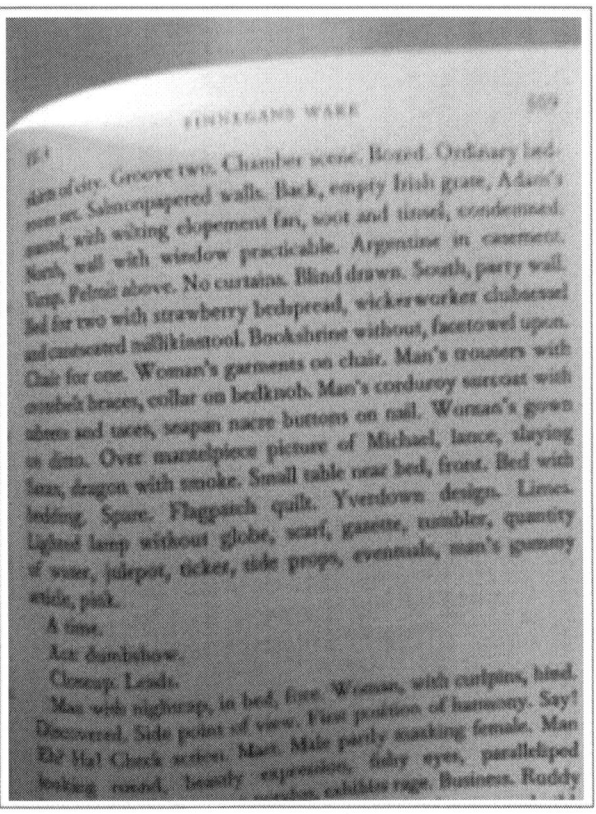

Mr and Mrs Porter are getting ready for bed. Mr Porter has a beastly expression and exhibits rage, whilst Mrs Porter's expression is *'haggish'*, depicting fear. There seems to be various attempts at an amorous advance from Mr Porter, at which point Mrs Porter runs off up a staircase with only one step whilst he passes out. She heads off to the children's bedrooms.

The Porters have a pet cat called Buttercup:

'Has your pussy a pessname? Yes, indeed, you will hear it passim in all noveletta and she is named Buttercup.'

Buttercup is described in similarly goddess-like terms to the mighty Biddy, of whom she is a good friend. Buttercup and Biddy pass the time gossiping about the family and customers at their pub.

Anyway, Jerry wakes up and Mrs Porter tells him not to wake Kevin and Isobel. Jerry has had a nightmare where his father was a very bad man – *'How shagsome all and beastful!'* Mrs Porter reassures him that it was all a dream and that there are no bad men in the house. She then rambles on about a myriad of things – from the church and fish to cycling and farting – before making reference to the late Finnegan and his wake.

Jerry eventually settles down and Mrs Porter returns to her bedroom. Mr and Mrs Porter then engage in a lengthy discussion about HCE, where his crimes are shown in yet another light. In this version, the ladies involved in the escapade in the park were encouraged by four men to spread rumours about him, on the basis that on the night in question he was so drunk that he wouldn't be able to remember what had happened. The ladies are presented in most unflattering terms and appear to have had many assignations with people they shouldn't. The particular bush where HCE lost his good name is in fact the bush of choice for local young lovers, which is interesting to know.

Talk then moves on to the court case, which was a confused affair where the judge and jury all disagreed about almost every aspect of the case. One of the witnesses requested musical accompaniment to her testimony, but was sadly refused by the Judge. They also muse upon Hosty's ballad and the fight in the pub when HCE's customers turned against him. Mr and Mrs Porter seem sympathetic towards HCE and blame all his problems on the fact he can't stand up to women. After a comical lecture about living a respectable life and the evils of sex, Mr and Mrs Porter copulate quietly so as not to wake the children. The chapter ends as coitus resolves when the cock crows and dawn breaks:

'O yes! O yes! Withdraw your member. Closure.'

Which is quite possibly the most underwhelming climax in literature.

Thoughts

Quite frankly, at this stage in proceedings I am just delighted that there is only one more chapter to go. This chapter is very much a return to form of Book 1, focusing on the crime in the park and the ambiguity of what really happened. For a while, I thought that the entire book was simply a dream conjured by young Jerry and I am still in two minds as to whether that is the implication. The Porters are a version of the Earwicker family, but who are seemingly untroubled by alcoholism and sexual deviancy. Perhaps a reminder not to judge others too harshly, as we are all human and prone to being at the mercy of our weaknesses. There are some wonderful passages laden with pathos and humour and this is one of the more straight forward sections of the book.

On to the final chapter! Will we finally discover the truth behind HCE and his bush-related endeavours? I'm not holding my breath…

Favourite Lines

'…every muckle must make its mickle,'

You can't expect someone else to take responsibility for your mickle.

    'So you be either man or mouse and you be neither fish nor flesh.'

I wonder what would happen if I said this to someone in real life.

    '...he being personally unpreoccupied to the extent of a flea's gizzard anent eructation, if he was still extremely offensive to a score and four nostrils' dilation,'

I'm not sure but I think this means that someone smells bad. Maybe.

BOOK 4 - THE FINAL CHAPTER

Everyone take a nice, deep breath – this is the final chapter! Although if you were hoping for any kind of resolution or explanation, you will be disappointed. In fact, as far as final chapters go, it is a little disappointing all round.

Book 4 (which consists of just one chapter) opens with an unknown narrator calling for dawn to break and the people of the world to awaken. Some sort of deity of the dawn talks nonsense for quite a while, mainly concerning inedible yellow meat, the twenty nine schoolgirls and fish. Someone goes away and then comes back again (possibly Shaun).

Eventually, Here Comes Everybody wakes up and is surprised that he has been dreaming. It has apparently been a long, hard night but now the day is coming and will make everything right again. A conflict or battle between night and day ensues, interspersed with details about the transient nature of rivers and the various regenerations of ALP. There is then some discussion about Shaun:

'Here's heering you in a guessmasque, letterman! And such an improofment! As root as the mail and as fat as a fuddle!'

'...night-shared nakeshift with the alter girl they tuck in for sweepsake.'

Shaun is then asked about the crime in the park and his involvement with ALP's letter. His vague reply states that anything can happen after night fall and only the deers know the truth for sure. Perhaps if we could find one of these deers, that might be helpful. But anyway. There is then a lengthy passage concerning the Kevin character, who seems to be a sanctimonious version of Shaun. Saint

Kevin becomes a priest and travels along rivers collecting Gregorian water. As you do.

Finally, day triumphs over night and a couple of jaunty chaps named Muta and Juva pop up and talk vaguely about beetles, a king and the story of HCE and ALP. They close with:

'Muta: May I borrow that hordwanderbaffle from you, old rubberskin?

Juva: Here it is and I hope it's your worming pen, Erinmonker! Shoot.'

A king and a tramp die. ALP seems to be trapped in a miasma of fairytales and dreams:

'That was the prick of the spindle to me that gave me the keys to dreamland.'

She is surrounded by *'Impossible to remember persons in unprobable to forget position places.'*

ALP now gives us her version of events and her thoughts on her letter. The much discussed (but never seen) letter apparently contained proof that HCE could not have committed the crime in the park, as he was canoodling with a lady named Lily under a grand piano at the time. She speaks surprisingly highly of her philandering husband – *'Meet a great civilian (proud lives to him!) who is gentle as a mushroom...'* Although, considering her own transgressions, an assignation under a piano seems pretty insignificant. We were warned earlier about the dangers of engaging in romantic pursuits with piano-playing lodgers, perhaps HCE should have been paying attention.

    The close of this chapter and, indeed, the book is given over to a plaintive monologue by ALP. She is attempting to wake HCE, who might actually be dead by this point. If he has given up the will to live, I can't say I entirely blame him. She tries to tempt him to awaken with suggestions of going abroad and she implores him to get up and put on his new big green belt. She then rambles on about *'two old crony aunts'*, who are reminiscent of both the gossiping washerwomen (one of whom turned into a tree) and the tale of the Mookse and the Gripes from Book 1.5. ALP is not fond of these two ladies, amusingly named Queer Mrs Quickenough and Odd Mrs Doddpebble. She also appears to randomly invent the world's favourite search engine:

'One chap googling the holyboy's thingabib and this lad wetting his widdle.'

I wouldn't advise googling this, but if you do, be sure to clear your search history. Anyway. ALP derides the two women and also the Four Masters. She firmly informs the unresponsive HCE that he must buy her a new girdle, before describing how she will distract herself from his failings by imagining him as an innocent young child – *'The child we all love to place our hope in forever.'* She is of the opinion that all men make mistakes and all people are prone to failure – *'It's something fails us. First we feel. Then we fall.'*

As ALP considers dying, she seems to forgive HCE and also herself and calls for a river to carry her home to the sea. The final line appears incomplete, but is in fact the opening fragment of the very first line in the book:

'A way a lone a last a loved a long the / riverrun, past Eve and Adam's, from swerve of shore to bend of bay, brings us by a commodious virus of recirculation back to Howth Castles and Environs.'

Thoughts

We did it!! Oh, we have done it, dear, sweet reader – we have completed *Finnegans Wake*! Of course, this is a mere glancing of the intricate and complex text and does not even begin to scratch the surface of this widely-studied work. With a book where almost every sentence is open to interpretation, it is likely impossible to provide a definitive synopsis. However, the impossible has always been a favourite of mine and I shall have a crack at an overview very shortly. In the meantime, I am off to have a lie down in a dark room – hopefully with a large steak and the biggest glass of wine you have ever seen in your life.

Favourite Lines

'(for the farmer, his son and their homely codes, known as eggburst, eggblend, eggburial and hatch-as-hatch can)'

The farmer and his son are keen on eggs, I see.

'He may be humpy, nay, he may be dumpy but there is always something racy about, say, a sailor on a horse.'

I have always thought this myself.

'Grand old Manbutton, give your bowlers a rest!'

I wonder if this has anything to do with the aforementioned bootybutton?

'A naked yogpriest, clothed of sundust, his oakey doaked with frondest leoves,'

This summer I shall be mostly wearing sun dust. (Also I wanted the final quote to involve nudity. And a priest.)

THE CONCLUSION - OF SORTS

We've done it! We have made it all the way through James Joyce's *Finnegans Wake*, a work that is widely labelled an unreadable work of genius. I am woefully under-qualified in the business of declaring genius, but I can certainly say that it isn't unreadable. I've just read it. It is – without doubt – incredibly difficult. It took Joyce seventeen years to write the bloody thing and one would assume that he knew what he was getting at, so for a mere mortal such as myself it was always going to be unlikely that I would gain any probing insights from just one reading. However, there are many elements that are obvious even to the most casual reader.

First off, in order to read *Finnegans Wake* you need to forget everything you thought you knew about literature. The hardest part of the whole process is abandoning the concepts of narrative, protagonists, plot and structure – Joyce has no truck with such things and trying to hang the text on a reliable framework is folly. This is a soundscape of noise that occasionally adopts a human voice, rather than any kind of prose. Also the notion of character is very fluid – we certainly have a key cast but they appear in many different forms, across varying timelines and displaying different behaviours. In some ways, this unreliability makes them seem more real than characters in a standard novel. So here they are, in all their demented glory:

Harold or Humphrey Chimpden Earwicker / Here Comes Everybody / HCE

Both the hero and the villain of the piece, HCE is certainly one of the most interesting literary characters I have come across. On the face of it, the story of HCE is one broadly of a fall from grace, a man who loses everything through drink and womanising. But then again we are never definitively sure exactly of his trespass, or even if it ever occurred at all. He has connections to the sea – he arrives in the book on a ship and there are several references to battles at sea and exploring. A drinker, gambler and womaniser, he has a dysfunctional relationship with his wife and family. Much is made of his downfall being related to drink and women, in particular his wife ALP. He is also representative of Adam (his downfall being similar in nature) and as an 'every man' character. He is both victim and offender, alive and dead, a gentleman and a monster. I suppose he really is sort of 'everybody'.

Anna Livia Plurabelle / ALP

Like her husband HCE, ALP is an extraordinary character. Seen as both a devoted wife and a shameless harlot, ALP is as much a victim of the events in the park as anyone, if not more so. The rumours of her husband being a rapist damage her reputation and she too becomes a target for the gossiping townsfolk. There are plenty of tales of her infidelities but she is also portrayed at times as a virginal, almost goddess-like character – although she does spend most of her appearances being somewhat hysterical. ALP is often associated with rivers, to the extend that she occasionally is a river. Quite a few people get drowned in rivers, come to think of it. Long-suffering housewife driven to distraction by her drunken husband's philandering ways, or heartless strumpet who destroyed HCE through her own selfish desires? ALP is the very best and very worst of all women. She and HCE make the perfect couple.

Shem The Penman

Son of HCE and ALP, Shem appears through the book at various stages in his life and in various guises. He is a writer and forger and it is generally thought that he wrote ALP's famous letter. Shem is a pitiful character and often mocked by his brother Shaun and others. Towards the end of the book there is suggestion that Shem is not in fact the son of HCE and this could be the cause of Shaun's irritation. I somehow ended up rooting for Shem, even though he appears to have no redeeming features whatsoever.

Shaun The Post

Shem's brother Shaun is apparently a postman but we only ever hear of him delivering one letter, and even that ended up with Biddy the hen. Shaun also has two sides to his personality. His alter ego Kevin appears to represent a youthful or unsullied version of

Shaun, who is otherwise brash, boastful, enormously fat and both revolting and hilarious at the same time. He is vicious to poor Shem but seems to share his father's love of the ladies. He never gives a straight answer to anything and his rambling responses to even the most innocuous of questions are often very funny. However, like his mother ALP, Shaun also has a pious persona, even going as far as to appear as Saint Kevin in the final book. He is the most unrepentant of sinners, unable to see his own shortcomings.

Isa / Izzy / Isobel

The younger sister of Shem and Shaun, Isa is probably the most disturbing character in the book. While her brothers appear as both young boys and also grown men, Isa seems permanently stuck in adolescence, although this does not stop her from having some very grown-up monologues. Rather than presenting as a metaphor for lost innocence, Isa comes across as never having possessed innocence in the first place, which is somehow worse. She is not a bad or unpleasant character, far from it. Her appearances are announced by the most dainty, Wonderland-esque prose but the general gist of her intentions is pretty dark. I cannot help wondering if Isa is representative of Joyce's own daughter Lucia, a lady plagued by mental illness to whom Joyce was inordinately close.

Biddy The Hen

Far and away my favourite character in the book. This humble hen is presented in exalted terms and is held in high regard by the townsfolk. Apart from being the finder of ALP's letter, Biddy is a symbol for one of the great, over-arching themes of the book – the circle of life. The various tales in the book go round and round, repeated and distorted throughout, with seemingly no beginning or end to any of them and characters are born, deceased and risen again on a fairly regular basis. The theme of 'chicken and egg' is prevalent – we are never sure what came first, what was cause and what was effect. But the greater purpose of existence itself is represented here by the mighty Biddy, at least that is my chosen interpretation, if only for the fact that at one point she considers raising a hen army. Now, you don't get *that* in many books.

There are various other characters that make several appearances – the gaggle of schoolgirls, Hosty the musician, Kate Strong the barmaid and of course Finnegan himself. There are also the twelve men who are both customers in HCE's pub and the jury in his court case, and the slightly sinister Four Masters who pop up here and there. I am absolutely convinced that the Duke of Wellington has something to do with it all, but I haven't been able to work it out. Endless people and places are constantly discussed, and sometimes people are places and sometimes they don't exist at all. Sometimes trying to work out who people are is simply a waste of time and it's just better not to know. As for the storyline, well – there isn't a story*line*. Stream of consciousness is one thing, but this is more of a four dimensional spiral of many stories seen from conflicting perspectives, interwoven with a matrix of random thoughts and ideas. Throughout much of the book there is a sort of 'background' commentary of absolutely everything and everything – science, history, religion, nature, politics, social ideology – it is almost as if Joyce just threw in bits of information that interested him at the time. The modern equivalent would be to have multiple browser tabs open and to click between them all, reading random bits of each. At times when people are being discussed, it is like scrolling through a social media newsfeed – unrelated snippets of people's every day lives, often making little sense to anyone who wasn't there at the time. Picking through all these many, seemingly random, things could distract one forever – although I dare say there are some fascinating insights behind all of them.

There is no linear narrative and we can never be sure of anything, but I will give you my best attempt at a synopsis:

ALP, a tailor's daughter, meets HCE upon a ship after his trousers are stolen. They fall in love and get married. After sailing around for a bit, ALP tires of life at sea and demands that HCE retires from adventuring and takes her to live in a pub in Dublin. There they produce three fairly disturbed children and settle down to either marital bliss or abject misery. Eventually, rumours start to emerge about HCE. He is suspected of committing a sexual indiscretion in the the park, although the versions of what actually happened range from the vicious rape of one or more girls, to nothing more than a cruel character assassination. ALP instigates a letter to be sent to everyone in town, either defending or deriding her husband. The letter doesn't make it to the intended audience, but is presented as evidence when HCE is tried in court. HCE is released from court, presumably being found innocent, but his friends and customers turn against him anyway. HCE then retreats from the world and maybe dies at the end. Meanwhile, everyone else drinks, gossips and fornicates, whilst gossiping about those who fornicate and drink.

Of course, I am barely able to scratch the surface of this magnificent tome. It is simultaneously a combination of all books (so many literary works are referenced I lost count – and probably missed countless more) whilst also being like no other book, ever. Words and language are both recklessly irrelevant and cunningly crafted and we have to look beyond them to appreciate what they actually represent. There are theories about the book being a dream sequence, taking place over the course of one night as a kind of sequel to *Ulysses*, or of being the work of a diseased mind – something Joyce actively encouraged at the time. It could be a retelling of the fall of man, or an elaborate commentary on infinity – the last line of the book joins up to the first and no conclusions are ever reached. Joyce has certainly achieved the coveted notoriety so desired by any writer, as people are not going to give up on the secrets of *Finnegans Wake* any time soon.

    Personally, I don't think that this book is written about any one thing. It is more a thing about which other books are written.

ABOUT THE AUTHOR

Lucy Brazier is a British writer and author. She enjoys hats, eating things and drinking tea. She is responsible for such crimes of literature as the *PorterGirl* series and daft political whodunnit, *Who Shot Tony Blair?*

PorterGirl - First Lady of the Keys
PorterGirl - The Vanishing Lord
PorterGirl - Sinister Dexter
Old College Diaries
Who Shot Tony Blair?
Finnegans What?

Printed in Great Britain
by Amazon